JEWEL OF THE MALL:
THE WORLD WAR II MEMORIAL

Introduction by Senator Robert Dole
Photographs by Stephen R. Brown

*DEDICATED TO **EDWARD AND JOAN BROWN**--*
THE GREATEST OF THE "GREAT GENERATION"

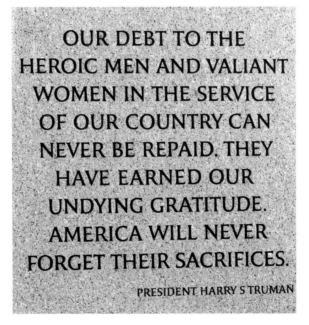

OUR DEBT TO THE HEROIC MEN AND VALIANT WOMEN IN THE SERVICE OF OUR COUNTRY CAN NEVER BE REPAID. THEY HAVE EARNED OUR UNDYING GRATITUDE. AMERICA WILL NEVER FORGET THEIR SACRIFICES.

PRESIDENT HARRY S TRUMAN

WWII MEMORIAL: JEWEL OF THE MALL
ISBN # 0-9766150-0-2
©Stephen R. Brown 2005

WWW.WWIIMEMORIALBOOK.COM
WWW.JEWELOFTHEMALL.COM

202-667-1965

PRINTED BY THE FOUNDRY
WWW.THEFOUNDRYCO.COM
MADE IN THE USA

THE **World War II Memorial** unifies the Mall joining the Washington Monument and Lincoln Memorial in a continuous vista. Entering from 17th Street, you are greeted with twenty-four bas relief panels depicting scenes from the Atlantic Front on the North side (right) and from the Pacific Front on the South side (left). Other bas relief panels depict pivotal stages in the War and on the Home Front. The 7.4 acre Memorial surrounds the refurbished Rainbow Pool. Two granite

Bas Reliefs copyright Raymond Kaskey Studio ©2003

pavilions enclose massive Eagle sculptures by Raymond Kaskey. At the western end, there is a wall of 4000 stars, one commemorating every one-hundred Americans who died in World War II. The fifty-six columns adorned with oak and wheat wreaths made of bronze represent the contribution of the states and territories towards the war effort. The pillars are joined by a bronze sculpted rope symbol-zing the bonding of a nation. The Memorial was designed by Friedrich St.Florian.

SENATOR ROBERT DOLE

In May of 2004, I joined thousands of fellow World War II veterans assembled on the Mall to dedicate another war memorial. Actually, that's not quite right. We don't build memorials to war—we build memorials to those who fight wars, to the millions who wear their country's uniform, to the even greater numbers on the home front who support them with their labor and their love, and to the precious freedom we fight to preserve.

We build memorials to offer instruction as well as inspiration. The lessons they teach are as relevant at Khe San and Khandahar as at Bataan, Gettysburg, or Valley Forge. Beginning with the most important lesson of war: trust your comrades as if your life depends on it, because it usually does. That's not all you learn on the battlefield. You learn that the blood spilled in conflict is all the same color, whether it comes from the sons of immigrants or the grandsons of slaves.

In a dangerous world, these are lessons that each generation must learn for itself. In the early years of the 20th century, my father fibbed about his age in the hope that he might go "Over There". In the wake of Pearl Harbor I joined the Army, and actually got "Over There". It was the children of the so-called Greatest Generation who went to Vietnam. They proved themselves every bit as great in their fidelity to freedom; even greater, in a sense. Those who fought in Vietnam risked every bit as much as the men of D-Day and Guadalcanal and did so without the political or popular support that we enjoyed.

In the words of Dwight D. Eisenhower, "I hate war as only a soldier who has lived it can, only as one who has seen its brutality and stupidity." On the one hand, war represents the ultimate failure of mankind. Yet it also summons the greatest qualities of which human beings are capable: courage beyond measure, loyalty beyond words, sacrifice and ingenuity, and endurance beyond imagining.

In the end, it is their sacrifice, their service and their blood that sanctify the Mall. They are forever remembered here, in the company of Washington, Jefferson, Lincoln, and Roosevelt. May this be a source of consolation and pride to the families who love them, the comrades who mourn them, and the vast numbers who draw inspiration from their example; may God watch over this proud company; and may God bless the United States of America.

Jewel of the Mall
By Stephen R. Brown

This book is dedicated to the "Greatest Generation" best exemplified by Senator Robert Dole. If he had not led the charge, I doubt the Memorial would have been finished or financed. Originally entitled "American Memory, American Vision," this book is also a tribute to the workers and artisans who completed this project in a mere two years. Their excitement was contagious. Their enthusiasm and ingenuity harkened back to the WWII effort on the Home Front. They made the impossible, possible.

My wonderful wife June and daughter Caitlin were supportive and enthusiastic throughout the project. Ray and Sherry Kaskey, Friedrich St.Florian, APEX Piping Systems, Laran Foundry, and construction superintendents David Tweedie and Barry Owenby made sure I had access to the site and cranes for photography. Nikon provided their finest cameras to document this historic project. Bogen Imaging provided additional illumination and support. Adobe Software was used to finish the photography and layout the book. Joyce McCluney, Senator Dole s "right hand", kept my spirits high when funds were low.

In June 2003, I noticed construction on the World War II Memorial was finally underway. I called sculptor Ray Kaskey to congratulate him and kidded him about his aversion to press and photography. He said: "No problem...there's been no press whatever."

After all the planning by major architectural and construction firms and historical and fine art committees, no one had thought about thoroughly documenting this historic project. And while this project had no end of financial and bureaucratic difficulties,

its historic and emotional appeal made it incumbent that I finish the book.

I first photographed the casting and manufacturing of the 80,000 pound bronze eagle sculptures at the Laran Foundry in Pennsylvania. In September 2003, APEX Piping Systems, which had designed the internal structure and columns for the eagles, did a "trial" installation inside the foundry. Because they needed several cranes to arrange the 80,000-pound sculptures, I set up large studio lights as far away from the action as possible and worked unobtrusively and carefully. In October and November, the eagles were shipped to Washington, and I was invited to document the installation of the eagles on the Mall.

It took three weeks to install the eight eagles and weld the laurel wreaths between them. I brought my safety harness and was given access to the cranes when the eagles were lifted into the air and lowered into place inside the Memorial Pavilions. During that period, veterans and their families were brought down to watch the installation of the eagles. Even the cranes had eagles painted on them. It was thrilling!

This book is both a portfolio of the finished Memorial and a historical documentation of the construction in granite and bronze. As the eagles

were lifted in the air against the D skyline, they seemed absolutely eno mous. Now that they are in place in th pavilions, they seem "right-sized".

As you wander the site in the late eve ning, you can experience the geniu of Ray Kaskey's high-flying eagle wreaths, rope and stars that adorn a chitect Friedrich St.Florian's majest design. As you look out through th columns representing the states ar territories that fought in World Wa II, they frame the other monumen on the Mall.

This Memorial is truly a masterpiec which I have come to see as the "Jew el of the Mall." Its classical desig intricate bronze work, fountains an seating arrangements invite the vis tor to rest and contemplate the pric of freedom.

My biggest thrill however, was th opportunity to write my father name next to the names of man other veterans on the inner structu of the Southeast Atlantic Eagle. H served in a PBY airplane -- a subma rine hunter -- off the Coast of Brazi He loved a difficult project and woul have been delighted to see this on completed.

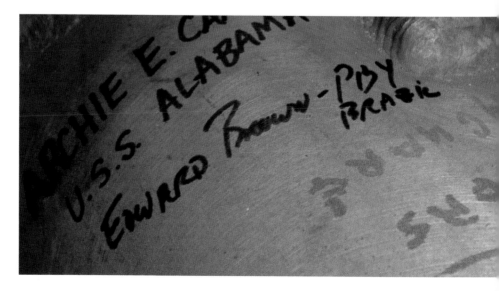

PACIFIC PACIFIC

HERE IN THE PRESENCE C
ONE THE EIGHTEENTH CE
THE NINETEENTH CENTU
WE HONOR THOSE TWENT
TOOK UP THE STRUGGLE
WAR AND MADE THE S
THE GIFT OUR FOREFA
A NATION CONCEIVED

GHINGTON AND LINCOLN,
Y FATHER AND THE OTHER
ESERVER OF OUR NATION,
CENTURY AMERICANS WHO
NG THE SECOND WORLD
IFICES TO PERPETUATE
RS ENTRUSTED TO US:
LIBERTY AND JUSTICE.

PACIFIC

THE WAR'S END
TODAY THE GUNS ARE SILENT. A GREAT
HAS ENDED. A GREAT VICTORY HAS BEEN
NO LONGER RAIN DEATH – THE SEAS BEAR O
MEN EVERYWHERE WALK UPRIGHT IN
THE ENTIRE WORLD IS QUIETLY

ATLANTIC

WE ARE DETERMINED
THAT BEFORE THE SUN SETS ON THIS
TERRIBLE STRUGGLE OUR FLAG WILL BE RECOGNIZED
THROUGHOUT THE WORLD AS A SYMBOL OF FREEDOM
ON THE ONE HAND AND OF OVERWHELMING
FORCE ON THE OTHER.

GENERAL GEORGE C. MARSHALL

"**WE ARE DETERMINED** THAT BEFORE THE SUN SETS ON THIS TERRIBLE STRUGGLE OUR FLAG WILL BE RECOGNIZED THROUGHOUT THE WORLD AS A SYMBOL OF FREEDOM ON THE ONE HAND AND OF OVERWHELMING FORCE ON THE OTHER."

-GENERAL GEORGE C. MARSHALL

BATTLE OF MIDWAY JUNE 4-7, 1942
"THEY HAD NO RIGHT TO WIN. YET THEY DID, AND IN DOING SO THEY CHANGED THE COURSE OF A WAR...EVEN AGAINST THE GREATEST OF ODDS, THERE IS SOMETHING IN THE HUMAN SPIRIT - A MAGIC BLEND OF SKILL, FAITH AND VALOR - THAT CAN LIFT MEN FROM CERTAIN DEFEAT TO INCREDIBLE VICTORY."

-WALTER LORD, AUTHOR

BATTLE OF MIDWAY   JUNE 4-7,
THEY HAD NO RIGHT TO WIN. YET THEY DI
DOING SO THEY CHANGED THE COURSE OF A WAR
THE GREATEST OF ODDS, THERE IS SOMETHING IN T
A MAGIC BLEND OF SKILL, FAITH AND VALOR–T
MEN FROM CERTAIN DEFEAT TO INCREDIBLE

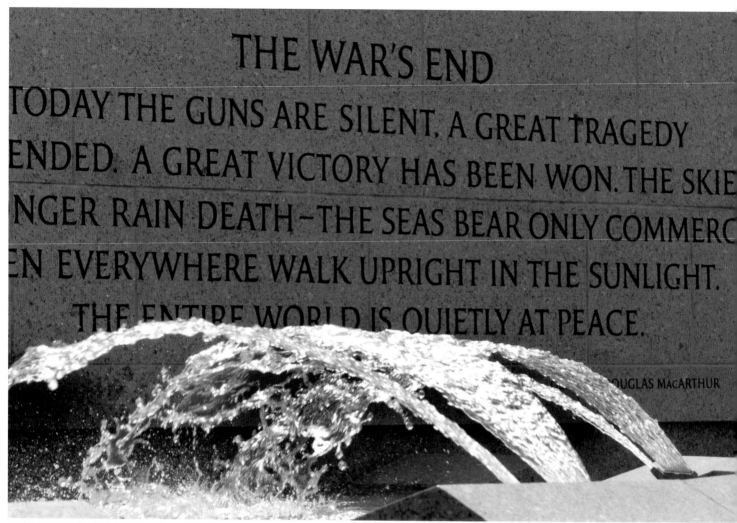

THE WAR'S END

"TODAY THE GUNS ARE SILENT. A GREAT TRAGEDY
HAS ENDED. A GREAT VICTORY HAS BEEN WON.
THE SKIES NO LONGER RAIN DEATH - THE SEAS BEAR
ONLY COMMERCE - MEN EVERYWHERE WALK UPRIGHT
IN THE SUNLIGHT. THE ENTIRE WORLD IS QUIETLY AT
PEACE."

-General Douglas MacArthur

HERE WE MARK THE PRICE OF FREEDOM
4000 SCULPTED GOLD STARS - ONE FOR EVERY 100
AMERICANS KILLED IN COMBAT - ADORN THE WESTERN
END OF THE MEMORIAL.

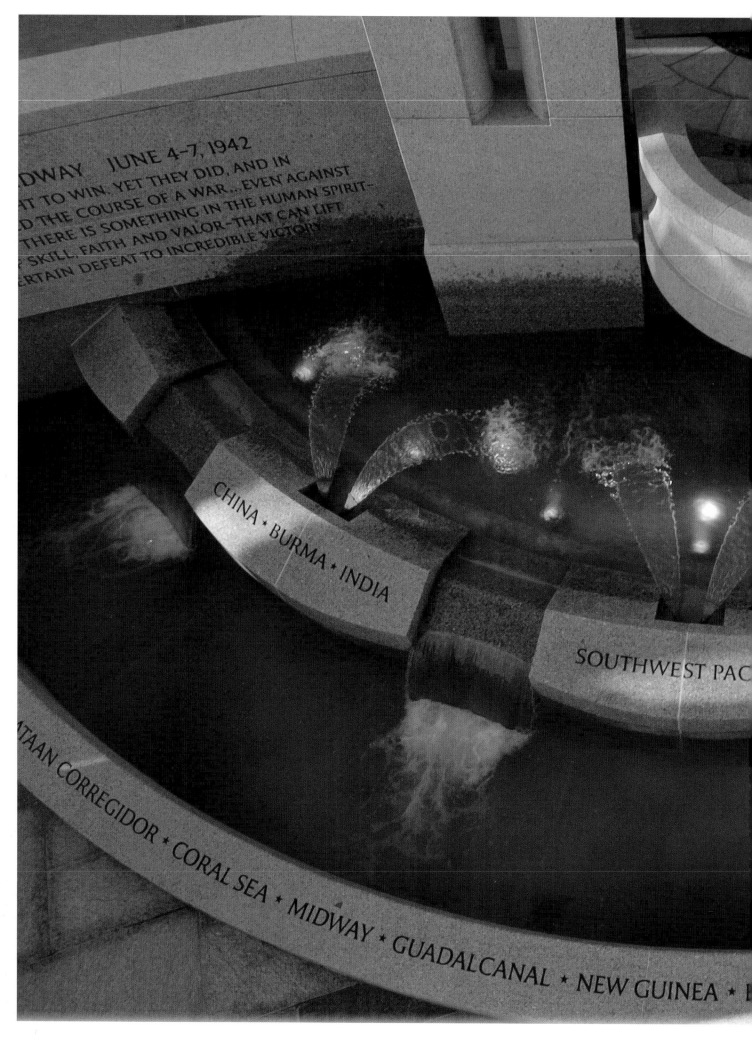

DWAY   JUNE 4-7, 1942
T TO WIN; YET THEY DID, AND IN
D THE COURSE OF A WAR...EVEN AGAINST
THERE IS SOMETHING IN THE HUMAN SPIRIT-
SKILL, FAITH AND VALOR-THAT CAN LIFT
ERTAIN DEFEAT TO INCREDIBLE VICTORY

CHINA ★ BURMA ★ INDIA

SOUTHWEST PAC

TAAN CORREGIDOR ★ CORAL SEA ★ MIDWAY ★ GUADALCANAL ★ NEW GUINEA ★

THE WAR'S END

TODAY THE GUNS ARE SILENT. A GREAT TRAGEDY
HAS ENDED. A GREAT VICTORY HAS BEEN WON. THE SKIES
NO LONGER RAIN DEATH—THE SEAS BEAR ONLY COMMERCE—
MEN EVERYWHERE WALK UPRIGHT IN THE SUNLIGHT.
THE ENTIRE WORLD IS QUIETLY AT PEACE.

GENERAL DOUGLAS MACARTHUR

NORTH PACIFIC

CENTRAL PACIFIC

PELELIU ★ LEYTE GULF ★ LUZON ★ MANILA ★ IWO JIMA ★ OKINAWA ★ JAPAN

★ TARAWA ★ KWAJALEIN ★ ATTU ★ SAIPAN TINIAN GUAM ★ PHILIPPINE SEA

MAKING A MEMORIAL

ARIZONA

OKLAHOMA

WYOMING

WASHINGTON

SOUTH DAKOTA

COLORADO

Friedrich St.Florian, Architect

THEY HAVE GIVEN THEIR
SONS TO THE MILITARY
SERVICES. THEY HAVE
STOKED THE FURNACES
AND HURRIED THE
FACTORY WHEELS. THEY
HAVE MADE THE PLANES
AND WELDED THE TANKS,
RIVETED THE SHIPS AND
ROLLED THE SHELLS.

PRESIDENT FRANKLIN D. ROOSEVELT

GUIDING LIGHTS:
Veterans Who Inspired the Memorial

STANLEY Wojtusik, 78, a Veteran of the Battle of the Bulge, contemplates the finished Memorial with satisfaction. His moving testimony in front of Congress inspired the passage of the long-overdue Memorial legislation.

OUR DEBT TO THE HEROIC MEN AND VALIANT WOMEN IN THE SERVICE OF OUR COUNTRY CAN NEVER BE REPAID. THEY HAVE EARNED OUR UNDYING GRATITUDE. AMERICA WILL NEVER FORGET THEIR SACRIFICES.

PRESIDENT HARRY S TRUMAN

Toby Felker (right) served with the Women's Airforce Service Pilots from 1943 to 1944 ferrying bombers. Her service inspired other women like Brigadier General Evelyn "Pat" Foote to serve in the Armed Forces. Foote served on the Memorial design committee.

WOMEN WHO STEPPED UP WERE MEASURED AS CITIZENS OF THE NATION, NOT AS WOMEN... THIS WAS A PEOPLE'S WAR, AND EVERYONE WAS IN IT.

COLONEL OVETA CULP HOBBY

RAY KASKEY, sculptor for the WWII Memorial, oversaw the largest bronze project in contemporary history. In a short two years, his studio produced four bronze columns, four bronze eagles and one bronze laurel wreath for each arch, twenty-four bronze bas reliefs for the ceremonial entrance, four thousand sculpted gold stars for the Freedom Wall, one-hundred and twelve bronze wreaths with armatures, fifty-two bronze ropes for the pillars, and the two flagpoles which mark the entrance to the Memorial.

AND TO END TYRANNY ★ AMER

MONUMENTAL DRAMA: Patrick Oakes and Scott Craig of APEX Piping Systems -- builders of the interio[r] skeleton and columns for the eagles -- guide the padded eagle into the South Pavilion. After the bronze skins wer[e] installed by Laran Foundry, the eight 20,000 pound eagles and laurel wreaths were transported to the Mall and very care[-] fully lifted into place using two cranes. The tension during this part of the installation was extraordinarily high. In th[e] end, the 20,000 pound eagle assemblies cleared the pavilion opening with three inches to spare.

FAMILY BUSINESS: John and Nick Benson of Rhode Island carved the quotations into the granite. They create a unique typeface for the WWII Memorial. The Bensons operate the oldest family-run business in the U.S. They designed and carved the type in stone for the Iwo Jima Memorial and the Kennedy Memorial in Washington, D.C. and the Civil Rights Memorial in Alabama. Joe Moss, a Master Stone Carver based in Annapolis, Maryland worked with them on this project, along with Christine DeMarco (bottom right), an apprentice carver from Rhode Island. She is staining the type with a lithochrome lacquer to highlight the letters. There are 3875 letters in the Memorial, all carved by hand.

PEARL HARBOR
DECEMBER 7, 1941, A DAT
WHICH WILL LIVE IN INFAN
NO MATTER HOW LONG
MAY TAKE US TO OVERCO
HIS PREMEDITATED INVAS
THE AMERICAN PEOPLE,
THEIR RIGHTEOUS MIGH
WILL WIN THROUGH
TO ABSOLUTE VICTOR
PRESIDENT FRANKLIN D. RO

HE WAR'S END
SILENT, A GREAT TRAGE
ORY HAS BEEN WON. TH
THE SEAS BEAR ONLY COM
LK U   S IN THE SUNL
R   IETLY AT PEACE.

GENERAL DOUGLAS

GRANITE was chosen for its aesthetic appeal, superior strength, durability, and water resistance. The two principal stones selected for the memorial are "Kershaw" for the vertical elements and "Green County" for the main plaza paving stone. "Kershaw" is quarried in South Carolina, while "Green County" is quarried in Georgia. Two green stones – "Rio Verde" and "Moss Green" – were used for accent paving on the plaza. Both are quarried in Brazil

"Academy Black" and "Mount Airy" were used to reconstruct the Rainbow Pool. "Mount Airy," quarried in North Carolina, is the original coping stone of the Rainbow Pool. An apron of "Academy Black", quarried in California, was used for the vertical interior spaces.

TRIAL INSTALLATION: APEX Piping Workers weld and bolt the eagles together during trial installations of the two sets of 32-foot high 80,000 pound sculptures. Three of the eagles (bottom right) stand awaiting the fourth eagle and laurel wreath to be lifted by crane and put in place. The 8000-pound laurel wreath (bottom right) is wrapped in a cold-forged piece of 2"x6" stainless steel and suspended by welds between the eagles' beaks. An X-ray

machine was used to inspect the welds. The bronze skin was treated with an aging chemical and burnished to give it uniform color.

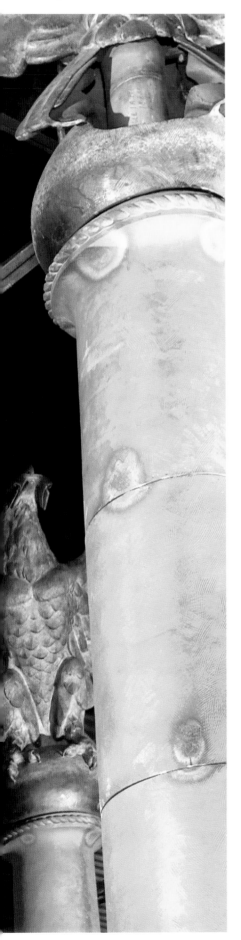

CASTING THE CHARACTERS: Sculptor Raymond Kaskey works with WWII re-enactors, Roland Blue and Brooks Tegler, in period uniforms. Kaskey poses them on a roundtable to prepare photographs from a variety of perspectives. The photos served as guides for the three dimensional creation of the bas reliefs. His assistants, Joanna Blake and Perry Carsley, (far right), carve the figures out of clay using the photographs for reference and then create a plaster of the relief. Each of the bas reliefs contains a minimum of 8 figures and took approximately 250 hours to sculp The drawings (below) were reviewed for historical accuracy and aesthetic appeal before any work could commence.

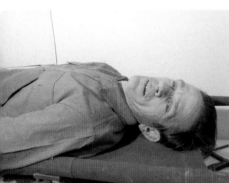

BRONZE CASTING: The plasters for the bas reliefs were shipped to the Laran Foundry in Pennsylvania where the clay molds were first poured into rubber molds (right) and then transferred to sand molds (bottom) and finally burnished (far right). When casting, bronze expands and contracts so the final measurements were a source of concern as the granite walls and frames of the Memorial were already in place.

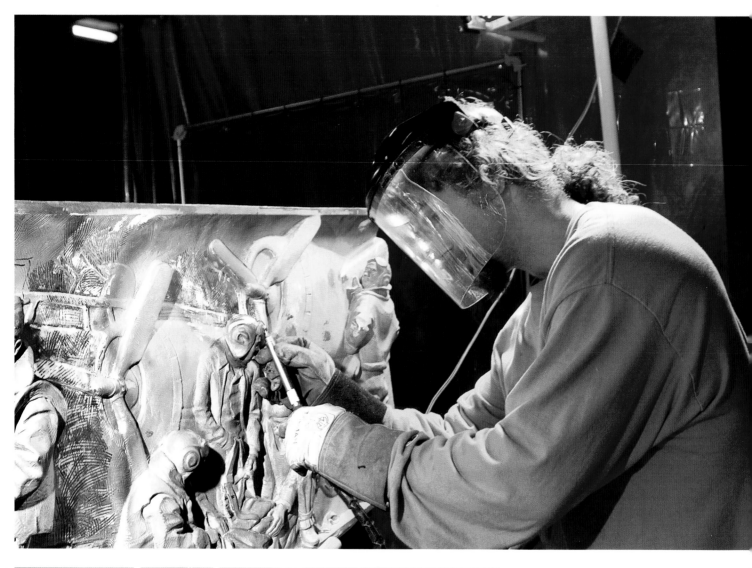

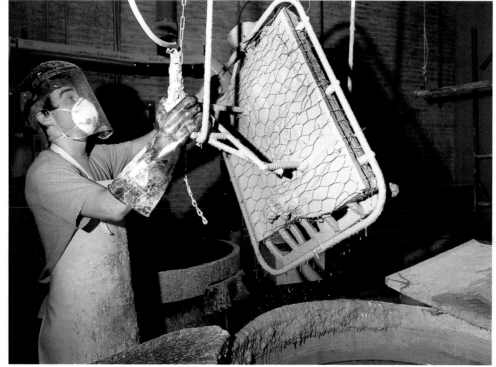

Memorial Overview

Authorization

President Clinton signed Public Law 103-32 on May 25, 1993, authorizing the American Battle Monuments Commission to establish a World War II Memorial in Washington, D.C, or its environs. It is the first national memorial dedicated to all who served during World War II and acknowledging the commitment and achievement of the entire nation.

Purpose

The memorial honors the 16 million who served in the armed forces of the U.S. during World War II, the more than 400,000 who died, and the millions who supported the war effort from home. Symbolic of this defining event of the 20th Century, the memorial is a monument to the spirit, sacrifice and commitment of the American people to the common defense of the nation and to the broader causes of peace and freedom from tyranny throughout the world. Above all, the memorial stands as a symbol of American national unity, a timeless reminder of the moral strength and awesome power of a free people united and bonded together in a common and just cause.

Site

The first step in establishing the memorial was the selection of an appropriate site. Congress provided legislative authority for siting the memorial in the prime area of the nation's capital that includes the National Mall. The National Park Service, the Commission of Fine Arts, and the National Capital Planning Commission approved selection of the Rainbow Pool site at the east end of the Reflecting Pool between the Lincoln Memorial and the Washington Monument. President Clinton dedicated the memorial site during a formal ceremony on Veterans Day 1995.

Design

Friedrich St.Florian, an architect based in Providence, R.I., was selected to design the memorial through an open, national competition in 1996. Leo A. Daly, an international architecture firm, assembled the winning team with St. Florian as the design architect. The team also included associate design architect George E. Hartman of Hartman-Cox Architects, landscape architect James van Sweden of Oehme van Sweden & Associates, sculptor Ray Kaskey, and stone carver Nick Benson. St.Florian's design concept was approved by the National Park Service, the Commission of Fine Arts and the National Capital Planning Commission in 1998. The three agencies approved the preliminary design in 1999, the final architectural design and ancillary elements in 2000, granite selections in 2001, and sculpture and inscriptions in 2002 and 2003.

Fund-Raising Campaign

The memorial was funded primarily by private contributions. Former Senator Bob Dole and Federal Express Corporation founder and CEO Frederick W. Smith led the fund raising campaign. The memorial campaign received more than $197 million in cash and pledges, only $16 million of which was provided by the federal government.

Construction

The memorial was built by the joint venture of Tompkins Builders/Grunley-Walsh Construction. The General Services Administration provided project management and contracting services to support the establishment and construction of the memorial and the Gilbane Building Company provided construction quality management services for the project. Construction began in September 2001 and the memorial was opened to the public in April 2004.

Dedication

The four-day dedication celebration was held Memorial Day weekend, from May 27-30, 2004. The official dedication ceremony was Saturday, May 29, 2004

ABMC

The American Battle Monuments Commission is an independent, executive branch agency with 11 commissioners and a secretary appointed by the President. The ABMC administers, operates and maintains 25 permanent U.S. military cemeteries and 25 memorial structures in 15 countries around the world, including three memorials in the United States. The commission is also responsible for the establishment of other memorials in the U.S. as directed by Congress.

World War II Memorial Design

The World War II Memorial design recognizes that the site itself pays special tribute to America's WWII generation. The memorial design creates a special place within the vast openness of the National Mall to commemorate the sacrifice and celebrate the victory of WWII, yet remains respectful and sensitive to its historic surroundings. The vistas from the Washington Monument to the Lincoln Memorial and the site's park-like settings are preserved, and the double row of elm trees that flank the memorial have been restored. Above all, the design creates a powerful sense of place that is distinct, memorable, evocative and serene.

Memorial Plaza

The plaza and Rainbow Pool are the principal and unifying features of the memorial. Two poles flying the American flag frame the ceremonial entrance at 17th Street. The bases of granite and bronze are adorned with the military service seals of all the military forces. A series of bronze relief panels along the ceremonial entrance balustrades depict America's war years.

Ramps at the north and south approaches provide access to the plaza; granite benches follow the curvilinear rampart walls.

Memorial Pavilions

Two 43-foot arched pavilions serve as markers and entries on the north and south ends of the plaza. Within each Pavilion is a "Baldachinos" or "canopy" which is an integral part of the design. Four American eagles hold a suspended victory laurel between their beaks to memorialize the victory of the WWII generation. Inlaid on the floor of the pavilions is the WWII victory medal surrounded by the years "1941-1945" and the words "Victory on Land," "Victory at Sea," and "Victory in the Air."

Pillars

Fifty-six granite pillars celebrate the unprecedented unity of the nation during WWII. The pillars are connected by a bronze sculpted rope that symbolizes the bonding of the nation. Each state and territory from that period and the District of Columbia are represented by a pillar adorned with oak and wheat bronze wreaths and inscribed with its name. The 17-foot pillars are open in the center for greater transparency, and ample space between each allows viewing across the memorial. The states and territories are placed in the order of their entry into the Union beginning at the Freedom Wall and alternating back and forth across the plaza.

Commemorative Area

Within the commemorative area at the western side of the memorial, the sacrifice of America's WWII generation and the contribution of our allies is recognized. A field of 4,000 sculpted gold stars on the Freedom Wall commemorates the more than 400,000 American who gave their lives. During WWII, the gold star was the symbol of family sacrifice.

Rainbow Pool and Waterworks

The historic waterworks of the Rainbow Pool have been restored and contribute to the celebratory nature of the memorial. The design provides seating along the pool circumference for visitors. Semi-circular fountains at the base of the two memorial arches and waterfalls flanking the Freedom Wall complement the waterworks in the Rainbow Pool.

Landscaping and Materials

Two-thirds of the 7.4-acre memorial site is landscaping and water, allowing the memorial to nestle comfortably within its park-like setting. The ceremonial entrance has three large lawn panels between the monumental steps. The double rows of elm trees have been restored and a replanting plan replaced unhealthy trees. A landscaped contemplative area is located at the northwestern corner of the site. Canopies of flowering trees augment re-seeded lawns.

The memorial is constructed of bronze and granite. Granite was chosen for its aesthetic appeal, superior strength, durability, and water resistance. The two principal stones selected for the memorial are "Kershaw" for the vertical elements and "Green County" for the main plaza paving stone. "Kershaw" is quarried in South Carolina, while "Green County" is quarried in Georgia. Two green stones – "Rio Verde" and "Moss Green" – were used for accent paving on the plaza. Both are quarried in Brazil. "Academy Black" and "Mount Airy" were used to reconstruct the Rainbow Pool. "Mount Airy," quarried in North Carolina, is the original coping stone of the Rainbow Pool. To enhance the aesthetic appearance of the water surface of the pool, an apron of "Academy black," quarried in California, was used for the vertical interior spaces.

Sculpture
- 4 bronze columns, 4 bronze eagles and 1 bronze laurel within each pavilion
- 24 bronze bas relief sculptures along the ceremonial entrance (12 on each side)
- 4,000 sculpted gold stars on the Freedom Wall
- 112 bronze wreaths with armatures (2 wreaths on each pillar, one on each side)
- 52 bronze ropes between the pillars

Dimensions
- Length (back of pavilion to back of pavilion): 384'
- Width (back of basin behind Freedom Wall to bottom of ceremonial entrance): 279'
- Plaza: 337' –10" long: 240' –2" wide; 6' below grade
- Rainbow Pool: 246' –9" long; 147' –8" wide
- Ceremonial entrance: 148' –3" wide; 147' –8" long (curb to plaza)
- 2 Pavilions: 43' above grade; 23' square
- 56 pillars: 17' above grade; 4' 4" wide; 3' deep
- Freedom Wall: 84' –8" wide; 9' high from plaza floor; 41' 9" radius

Bas-Relief Panels

A series of bas-relief sculpture panels created by sculptor Raymond Kaskey were set into the balustrades of the north and south ceremonial entrance walls. The bas-reliefs consist of 24 separate panels. The 12 on the north depict the Atlantic front; the 12 on the south depict the Pacific front.

The unifying theme of the panels is the transformation of America caused by the country's total immersion in World War II. The panels depict the all-out mobilization of America s agricultural, industrial, military and human resources. This transformed the country into the arsenal of democracy as well as the breadbasket of the world.

The visual inspiration for these panels is the bas-relief sculptures that encircle the Pension Building in Washington, D.C., which were influenced by the bas-reliefs on the Parthenon. What these bas-reliefs have in common is that all are "isocephalic", a Greek word meaning that the heads of the principal figures line up horizontally. The human scale is the unifying element common to all 24 panels. All details, scenes, equipment, etc, are subordinated to the scale of the figure. The unity of purpose unique to this time in America is best evoked by placing the visual emphasis on the individual in this time-honored manner. Most of the panels are based on historical photos.

Atlantic Front Panels

Lend Lease
Bond Drive
Women in Military
Rosie the Riveter/Aircraft Construction
Battle of the Atlantic
Air War/B-17
Paratroopers
Normandy Beach Landing
Tanks in Combat
Medics in Field
Battle of the Bulge
Russians meet Americans at the Elbe.

Pacific Front Panels

Pearl Harbor
Enlistment
Embarkation
Shipbuilding
Agriculture
Submarine Warfare
Navy in Action
Amphibious Landing
Jungle Warfare
Field Burial
Liberation
V-J Day

***Information compiled from fact sheet issued by the American Battle Monument Commission

Eagle Remnants after casting at Laran Foundry, Pennsylvania

NOTES

NOTES